STREAMLINE
HOW TO TEACH YOURSELF MONEY
FINANCIAL EDUCATION

KWABENA OBENG DARKO

STREAMLINE

© Kwabena Obeng Darko
October, 2020

E-mail your questions and comments to the author at:
info@odtrah.com.gh

Designed and Printed and Published by:

Odtrah
P . O . BOX KN 5668
Kaneshie-Accra.
GHANA.
TEL: 233 24 6631874

All rights reserved. No part of this publication may be reproduced, stored in a retrieval system, or transmitted in any form or by any means, electronic, mechanical, photocopying, recording or otherwise without prior permission of the publisher.

STREAMLINE
HOW TO TEACH YOURSELF MONEY

FINANCIAL EDUCATION

KWABENA OBENG DARKO

DEDICATION

I dedicate this book to those who believe in personal financial education and are helping people with this kind of education.

AUTHOR'S NOTE AND ACKNOWLEDGMENT

I am thankful to my mentors, parents, siblings and friends for their love and kindness. To my wife, Marie and children, Yaa, Awuraa and Kwabena, I love you always.

CONTENTS

Dedication 4
Acknowledgement 5
Introduction..7

Chapter 1. Stabilise yourself 15

Chapter 2. Personal financial education................................21

Chapter 3. Wrong Money Data 29

Chapter 4. Have financial goals..33

Chapter 5. Financial Training...39

Chapter 6. Financial Growth..45

Chapter 7. Money Equality..51

Chapter 8. Family and financial education............................59

Chapter 9. Sell for your financial freedom............................65

Chapter 10. House Ownership and Your Finances.............71

Chapter 11. Streamline Your Finances 75

Afterword 79

INTRODUCTION

The world as we knew it changed in 2020 when COVID-19 disrupted our economies and movements but not so much in Africa. It has never become more important to financially educate ourselves like now. It requires a stronger understanding of money, and how we relate with money, job and career. Around the world many would lose their jobs and many businesses would have to change their approach of doing business. If your business is still profitable or even exists at the end of 2020, you have really done well. Money and what we call investment would change going forward. Those of us in Africa have not been that affected as we have not really been part of this global prosperity bubble. Our economy is largely pay as you go. Individuals don't run on credit. Different skillsets and an upgraded understanding of money will be needed to be part of the prosperity of Africa.

Growing up, we thought to become rich meant;
- Going to school
- Travelling to some of these countries that have been packaged as wealthy
- Having a good job
- Occupying a big government position

We were conditioned with that script which most of you will agree is not necessarily true. We will need proper teachings about money to build financial success.

Few grow up with the right understanding of money, how it is acquired, how it is preserved and how it is multiplied. For many of us, our knowledge of money is limited to how to work to get salary and how we use it to get the basic necessities of life. Others are told that their prosperity is in the hands of another person, their government or their church. When reality hits, then they discover the truth that their prosperity is in their own hands.

Building houses or buying cars do not mean we are rich. Building a house and owning a car is beating poverty. Beating poverty and being rich are not necessarily the same. A lot of people have houses and cars but have no structure, business, or investment that makes them money consistently. Wealth creation is systemic. The mindset of the rich is different from the mindset of the poor or the average. Right financial knowledge brings financial prosperity. The rich think differently about money.

Again, financial knowledge as a necessary tool to build financial systems in solving economic problems and being rewarded is something we have to be aware of.
For those of us who don't come from well-to-do families, it is likely that our money data is wrong and this is seen in the

choices and decisions we make when we get money.

As they say, we can only do better if we know better. So most of us don't do better financially because our financial knowledge is no better. This knowledge is responsible for the financial skills we have built over our life-time. The good thing is that if we get the right knowledge and put it into practise, we acquire the needed skills which will be responsible for the financial results we get.

- If we continually struggle with debt, it means our financial decisions are not rightly thought out.
- If we cheat and lie to get money, it means our financial data is wrong.
- If we spend all that we have on consumables and have nothing saved or invested for the future, it means we don't have the right financial knowledge or skill.
- Those with the right financial skills are good with cash flow, financial planning, daily financial choices, expenses, income, loans and their repayment with interest, how our financial institutions work, and many more.

The answer is in the right acquisition of the right money data, that is, the principles of money, and more importantly, puting them into practice.

Everything about our money life rests on the money data we have. If it is good, our choices will be good and if it is bad, our money choices will be bad.

Everyone uses money and yet, very few of us read or study about money and that is why many of us struggle with money. This is why it does not matter our;

- level of education
- kind of profession
- salary bracket

If the money data is wrong, it becomes difficult to take full responsibility of our finances. There are laws and principles that guide everything in this world. If we don't know or understand the principles that apply under any specific situation, we will make mistakes. We cannot grow until we get the right fundamentals, and the pathway of growth is painful and disheartening.

It is important to know that, without very intentional, constructive, focused and consistent education on money, we will not be properly informed on money. We will just have an opinion on money and we don't become prosperous with just an opinion about money. Our concept of money will determine whether we will lack or have money as we go through life. There are so many problems in life but the money problem should not be part of them. Sadly, it is the number one problem many people have.

We worry about money all our lives because of what we know or don't know about money.

I have shared in this book some basic personal understanding on money and how any of us can move from a state of struggle, to being able to develop the right mindset, skillset and the needed sense of personal financial responsibility to create a better financial life and future. Life is continually upside down until we build the right skills. Some will build businesses and some will work for those who build businesses or the government, but whatever it is that you do, if you have the right financial skills, you will be able to build the financial future that will help you to;

1. enjoy life
2. help many people
3. live your dreams and aspirations.

You don't have to sell your soul to do this. You can keep your values and still have financial freedom and be truthful in your dealings. You don't have to be a crook to have money. Financial success is in us having the right financial skills and taking responsibility in building our personal financial systems and following them through. God has already blessed us with every resource needed to be successful. Examples are, our talents, our natural drives, energy, relationships, natural resources, brains, etc. It is up to us to make things happen and if we fail to do so, we should not blame anybody for this; not the government, God, the devil or whoever.

Our only problem will be our ignorance of this reality; the reality that God has already BLESSED us and so if you have financial problems, it does not mean you are cursed. It is very likely to be financial ignorance.

We can only be controlled when we allow someone to control;
1. Our mind
2. Our time
3. Our money (other resources)

Our intelligence is developed by the questions we ask and the more we are able to critically think. That is why you should never let anything take charge of your mind and what feeds it.

Take note of religious teachings that undermine the value of how powerful your mind is when it is well developed. Your life reflects the state of your mind and how you have nurtured that mind.

Read books on money, at least a book every month and practise it. Don't leave your financial well-being to chance, lottery or miracles. The mind is a very powerful tool God has given us and if we lose it, we lose our very existence. If you go to a room full of gold bars and the room is dark, you will not know that the room is full of treasures until you put on the light. The light does not put the gold bars there, it just reveals them. It is the same thing with the treasures we have within us; it takes the right light to reveal them. That light is knowledge. The intensity of the knowledge determines the intensity of the light we have.

God is not the one responsible for your finances. It is possible to have wrong data on money because of wrong teachings, where you are told to wait for money. The richest in this world did not become rich by waiting. They worked and applied the right money teachings.

Money follows prudent economic decisions and activities. Lazy people are soon poor, hard workers get rich (A wise man once said). It is said that no one builds a house and does not sit down to count the cost first.

Similarly, if you want to build financial success, sit down and count the cost. Jesus said that wisdom is justified by her children. If your financial results are not what you want, then check the financial wisdom you have. God is not the one doing the work, you are. Your financial success is not with anyone. It is with you and it is your sole duty. Religion plays a huge role in the lives of Africans. We only have to practice religion with the right values for humans. Love.

Hope. Faith. Respect. Kindness.

What we invest our time in is what we reap. We cannot waste our time on frivolities and think that we will get our money organized. Those who are able to take charge of their finances take charge of their time as well. We all have 24hours a day. What we put in that time is what we become.

Most people use 8-10 hours of those hours to sleep and about 8-10 hours to work and the 4-6 hours to do other things. Those who are able to leverage their time well on things that make them progress in their finances are those who succeed with their finances. Your future is where your money goes. Where we spend or invest our money is where our future financial status will be. So be intentional about how you spend your money and your time. Spend money to get the right financial knowledge that will help you to build the right financial skills. The investment you make in educating yourself financially is the best financial investment.

In this book, I hope to add to your financial awareness and communicate how important it is for us to have the right money data. This will help to develop the right financial skill to build the great future we all desire, especially when it comes to Africans/Blacks. Our orientation on money will help us to develop our lives, families, companies, countries, and the continent as a whole. Let us continue.

CHAPTER ONE

STABILISE YOURSELF

It takes a lot to live as a black person or an African in this world. The global power structure has been set to make us poor, maltreated and marginalized. This began when the Europeans set their foot on our beautiful continent for economic gain. It is hard to be Black or African and not be traumatized by vile images of poor African children who need help on TV. At the same time, Western countries are promoted as paradises. No wonder Africans see other African countries as poor and think that to make it, we must go to those countries packaged on TV to us as successful.

> *The African image has been annihilated and humilted through their religion, science, politics etc.*

Social media, particularly Youtube, is helping us to realize these lies. There is a huge difference between the mindset of Africans born and bred in Africa and those born outside Africa. *Most of us born in Africa have been programmed to see the Whiteman as a savior; as a matter of fact, Jesus has been made white and the Devil has been made black.*

Evil things are tagged black and it has affected the way we Africans see ourselves. Regardless of the level of our education or status in society, if those subconscious biases are not dealt with, they become destabilizing weight on the soul of the African or Black person. Look at how Africans or Blacks who live in these so called developed countries are treated economically, socially, politically and even in terms of wealth and power. I am not referring to individuals, but the economic power structure that hugely benefited from slavery and colonization and what the image of Africans or Blacks has become as a result of that. We Africans are hardly connected to anything science, technology, innovation, and the likes, but very easily linked to entertainment and sports. *You have got to get new data on your race as an African if you want to create that financial future in your country in Africa.*

We can all see the rate at which West Africans in particular are eager to travel to the West for economic gain. This is because we believe that we can go to these countries and succeed financially in spite of our lack of knowledge on the principles of money.

It is a dangerous mental programming that was brought to us through slavery and colonization. We can travel, but to believe that we must travel to have a fair chance of financial success is proof of our ignorance of how wealth is created systematically. To be able to have the courage and selfconfidence to go through the processes to build our own wealth as Africans, we should be stabilized with the right information on our history and race and be able to maneuver through the world systems that have positioned us Africans at the bottom of the economic ladder.

Nothing is as powerful as a self-confident African who is proud of his/her heritage, skin, hair, clothes, culture, etc.

I have seen very well educated Africans who are frustrated about the prospects of Africa because they have not intentionally studied or read the African subject from African scholars who believe in Africa and its prosperity, dignity and future. I had to be stabilized with the right knowledge and that was when my confidence in myself and the continent got corrected.

I then started to be constructive and intentional about all the beauty and the positivity in living and building in Africa without wanting to live anywhere else. I stopped feeling frustrated, complaining and blaming the government, corruption or leadership for my problems.

Pan African education is the secret. It is very difficult to be a proud African who believes in the economic empowerment of Africans without being Pan African. I am determined to be part of the solution in bringing awareness and prosperity to our people and our Continent. That is where real fulfilment is. That is how I think we are going to make a difference in the lives of our people. Living purposefully. We have got to stabilize emotionally, mentally and spiritually as Africans by acquiring the right information to build our self-image and confidence.

Pan African education positions the African to be aware of the scientific, technological, managerial, engineering, political and other achievements of Africans and people of African descent. By the time we are through the western type of education we are given in Africa, we are no longer committed to the cause of developing our people and the continent until we get the other education which comes through Pan African education. This did the trick for me. I started to believe in Africa and our prosperity. It elevates one above blaming corruption, bad leadership and the problems that western education has programmed us to focus on.

Fundamentally, Africa has been founded to be economically weak. The continent was patitioned into small countries without any proper economic power. Just consider how our education systems and government structures are run, in addition to how the institutions of this world behave towards the continent. Getting the proper Pan African education will correct something in you as African or a descendant of Africa.

This brings understanding to all. Study the history of Africa for the last 1000-6000 years, at least. Never believe that there is something wrong with you because you are black. That is a lie. Don't believe that history that they have told us that made us victims. *We are kings and queens of a wealthy heritage. Believe in yourself.*

Our heroes said this; that as long as you are black, you are an African, and you are intelligent and beautiful. It is that important.
Stabilise.

CHAPTER TWO

PERSONAL FINANCIAL EDUCATION

Personal financial education is the ability to have the right fundamental knowledge and skillset to make the right decision on your finances. The absence of it leads to poor financial choices and debt. There is the need to understand money, how it is acquired, multiplied and preserved. Personal financial education also helps to process and plan our financial future well. That is;

Personal financial education equips us to build our own financial systems.

1. How we handle our money daily
2. How we budget
3. How we save money
4. Our understanding of cash flow and investments
5. How we understand the tax laws . And many more.

Our financial education is responsible for how we even handle our business finances as entrepreneurs and if it is weak, we create a mess. *It is difficult to build a successful businesses if our financial education is poor and weak.*

It is the kind of education that is hardly taught in our schools. We are taught how to get good exam reports and how to become successful in getting jobs and getting salaries, but not how to become rich.

My mother's father could neither read nor write, and would be called an illiterate in today's terms. Interestingly, he was so astute with his finances that by way of preparing for retirement, he stored a huge mountain of sand on his land while working as a transport operator and a cocoa farmer. He started to sell off his investments when he retired from his business which took care of him until he died and even left some to his children.

How did he get that much financially educated such that, he did not die poor while formally educated professionals sometimes die poor? It's because personal financial education is not acquired in the classroom. That is why our business people operating in our markets (example Makola or Adum) have more money than most of our educated people who depend on monthly salaries. If you doubt it, ask your friends who work at any of our banks. I subconsciously captured my grandfather's resourcefulness. He had sheep, goats, chicken, an orange farm etc., which he operated commercially. He was a great man and yet he never stepped in a classroom. He wanted to see us all go to school and had a black board in his house which we all used to study.

He had his flaws but he was very intelligent and hard working. My grandmother too was a trader and a farmer who seemed to have cash on her every day. *It appears to me that the more we spend time in formal education, the less financially intelligent we become.* We are made to believe in our certificates more than our abilities. We become financially fearful and lazy, less critical in thinking and less skilled in solving problems. The type of education we are given in Africa makes us depend on the government or others financially.

That is why we have to personally educate ourselves financially. *If you play with personal financial education and its importance, to get money, you will have to become a criminal or a thief.* It is possibly one of the reasons why we have corruption widespread in the areas our educated people work. They just don't know how to make money on their own. Most of us don't get this education from home, school, church or the general culture. Perhaps, it's the reason why most of us make

> Nothing is as powerful as a self-confident African who is proud of his/her heritage, skin, hair, clothes, culture, etc.

wrong decisions with money and struggle financially all our lives. The world has programmed us to waste time on fun, ceremonies and things which do not improve us in terms of productivity and finance.

I remember when I started to read about money, entrepreneurship, finances, investments and others business and management books as an engineering student at Kwame Nkrumah University of Science and Technology, people questioned me. They wondered why an engineering student would be reading things about money and not on machines. What they probably did not know was that money would be needed to build and run the machines. What they did not know was that the one who had financial education was better equipped to control money and eventually employ them to build and run those machines. I was educating myself financially.

It took me between ten to fifteen years to have an adequate understanding of money without which I would not have taken the path of entrepreneurship. Even with this continuous learning about money, I ended up making so many mistakes with my finances particularly at the business level; taking wrong loans with huge interest rates, taking wrong projects and lots of wrong financial decisions.

Some people on the other hand have far better financial skills because they have the right money data. This helps them in their personal and business finances which results in prudent financial decisions with less financial troubles and challenges. They make good decisions on expenses like wages, purchasing of products, projections and budgeting, rent payment, cash flow, prioritizing of resources etc. The level of our financial education shows in the quality of decisions we make financially. If it is weak, we suffer and if the financial education is strong, we are able to make the right decisions in our finances either as individuals or as entrepreneurs. My recommendation is that you make your own timetable on the type of financial education you want to give to yourself, that is:

- The number and the types of books you want to read on finances every month
- The types of seminars you want to attend
- The videos on YouTube or audios you want to train with every month.

The better our financial content, the better the financial skills we are able to build over time. This type of education is one of the best decisions we will have to make in life, because if we don't have good control over our finances, virtually every other area of our lives is likely to be disorganized. Money has great impact on all the other aspects of our lives, be it marriage, health, influence in society and so on.

There is no point in debating how important money is in this life. Where you live, the car you drive, where your children go to school, your health, etc., all have direct correlation with how much of money skills and education you have. Don't tell me that most people are happy and fulfilled when they cannot pay their children's school fees, cannot pay their debts and hospital bills, and cannot help people who are in need though they dearly want to support. So intentionally study money, how it is acquired, kept and invested. *The streams of income we are able to build show our level of financial expertise.*

Most people seem to think that building houses and buying cars show that they have money. *People think consumption is the same as production.* Those with money have more being produced than being consumed and so have much excess. It's the reason why they have money. They have learned to build structures and systems around their financial activities through businesses and various investment tools.

It seems to me that people with great financial skills buy nice houses and cars out of the residue that their businesses and investments bring. *You have got to be in charge of your finances.* Don't leave it in the hands of the government or your employer. God gave us gold, oil, diamond etc. together with our brains so that we can turn them into useful products.

There are a lot of institutions that will come for your money if you are not awake. They come in various shapes and forms - religious bodies, the government, the media and colleges offering all kinds of courses just to collect money from you without any direct benefit. Once you become aware, you will stop following the hope they sell to you.

Don't let anyone use superstition and magic to keep collecting your money. Money is not magic or miracle. Watch your beliefs on money. If you so believe you were born not to have any money, it will be so and if you believe you deserve the best of life too, it will be so if you work it.

Money is not evil. It is neutral. It depends on the character of the person who has it - whether good or bad. It has saved many people's lives because they could pay their hospital bills. Money has also brought joy to people because someone could buy them a house or a car or send them to school.

Personal financial education
Personal financial education is super critical to how we handle money and whether we are going to be able to create any or not. Be very deliberate about this kind of education.

CHAPTER THREE

WRONG MONEY DATA

The type of data we have and use control our choices. Most people's data on money is wrong and that is why they struggle with money all their lives. Many of us don't define financial success by the number of sources of income that we have, which must be more than what we spend in a given time.

People wrongly define financial success as children going to good school or having a well-paying job.

Money talks

While growing up, I knew of a certain lively man who would go to every funeral and dance to every song played. He was very popular. *He was someone people loved.* He was very hardworking and very sincere, straightforward and blatant. *His problem was that every time that he got paid, he would gather friends and they would go and have fun.* When asked why he withdrew so much money at a time, he would say that he heard the money talking to him as soon as he was alerted that his salary had hit his account.

The money was saying "fiw" "fiw" like a bird tweeting. Often, boys would time him on pay day for him to spend on them. He would stuff his salary in his pocket and go on a spending spree on his crew.

Money is not feeling
This man struggled with money because he listened to money talking to him whenever he received his salary and he was a bit emotional about money as well. He would give his money to people who preyed on his kindness and others would even steal his money. As you can guess, he did not save money and he obviously did not invest his money. *He had financial problems, because he had wrong money data.*

Majority of Africans who live abroad will spend all their lives doing all types of jobs and will send money to build huge houses of about 12 bedrooms in Africa which they will not even come to live in. Sometimes, family members will occupy those houses and the owner will still be sending money from abroad to pay bills. They will still be working long hours with multiple jobs even in their old age and still be struggling financially. If there is a health crises or any major life issue, they are not able to take care of themselves financially. Financial independence becomes out of reach. That is wrong money data.

We mostly save money to build houses, buy cars, pay school fees or for occasions such as weddings or funerals. *We should consider investing the money in cocoa farms, businesses, building houses for rent or investing in anything that will multiply the money before we use the money for whatever we desire.*
Wrong money data will make us;

- Borrow and not pay
- Trick people to get money without being conscious of the ramifications.
- Cheat people of the money that they have worked hard for and think we are smart.

Wrong money data will make us believe that we need someone to give us capital before we start our business. It makes us wait for a long time for the 'right' job which will pay us good money, instead of starting from where we are with the little we have.

Wrong money data makes people believe that God is responsible for their financial future or the devil is the reason for their financial struggles. People with wrong money data are the ones looking for anointing oil, prayers, and prophetic ways to get financial success. Hard work pays. It is a process.

Wrong money data makes people believe that when their

party comes to power, they will be rich. They are the ones looking for big money and usually don't have regard for the small money they get daily.

Most people with wrong money data believe some courses in the university will make them rich. Wrong money data makes people believe that they will be rich once they travel out of Ghana.

Until we correct our wrong money data, our struggles with money will be a lifelong battle. Showing off money and impressing people with it while we find it difficult to sleep because of financial constraints that come out of our inability to pay our debts, is proof of wrong money data. Go against wrong money data.

CHAPTER FOUR

HAVE FINANCIAL GOALS

Until you are ready to sacrifice to achieve the goals you have, you are not ready for them. It will take honesty, faithfulness, hardwork, gratitude, kindness, sales skills, etc. to get to your financial goals. What kind of person must you become to get to your financial goals?

Your Goals require steps

Never give up on yourself when things get tough. Nothing predicts the future of your finances or your life more than how you spend your money, time and energy today, as against the financial goals you have set for yourself and the detailed plan you have to get to those goals. *There will be problems before you achieve your financial goals.*

There will be difficulties. Life is full of troubles.

Our Financial Ecosystems
People have been limited in their conditions, knowledge, and in the environment that prevent them from living their unlimited successful financial lives. You are unlimited so long as your goals are concerned. The only limiting factors are those you set for yourself. Achieving anything is tough without the right preparation. *We have not been given enough strong knowledge and skills, and so people underestimate the necessary inputs and therefore get exhausted along the journey.* The best of our teachers only give moderate inspiration and motivation.

Believe that those financial goals are possible. You have got to be brutally honest to yourself. This will help you to achieve your financial goals. So don't leave your financial wellbeing to chance. The challenges in life are many and people have little or no knowledge, skill and resource to continue to push till they are successful. For this reason, many give up on their financial goals or cut corners to achieve them.

When we started our construction companies, we were confronted with so many challenges which could have made us stop. We were willing to do things to support others and our country. Problems came from every corner - employee issues, debt, nonpayment for projects, etc. Our finances were in bad shape for years. We were not skilled and not networked. The country's economy was not good, construction materials prices were doubling in months and the dollar against the cedi was very volatile. We also had business partnership problems, lack of clarity with respect to what to do, taking high interest loans that we were not ready for, and many other issues. These put so much pressure on our financials. It took us close to ten years to get out of the overstretched financial problems that my lack of precise financial decisions brought.

Your leverage is self-development
The numerous problems did not matter as much as we were committed to continuous self-development. I had to read books on finances, entrepreneurship, business relationship, Africa, etc. Watched so many videos on YouTube, read lots of articles online, continuously listened to audios in my car, at home etc. That is how we stayed above the challenges and the noise. I do this all the time - watching or listening to materials on entrepreneurship, finance, self-development, etc. We need knowledge to keep going. Don't play with this.

Self-education is the key to get ahead in life and reach our goals, yet many are waiting for someone somewhere to help them to realize their financial goals. Don't do that mistake. Go with what you have and keep developing yourself. The road will be difficult, but keep going. Relationships will break, you will be accused and you will lose opportunities, sales, money, contracts, businesses, etc.

All these will prepare you for the task ahead. Don't waste time to pray away difficulties and problems. *Your ability to solve problems will be that which separates you from people.* Solve financial problems. That is how we get out of financial difficulties. *Don't cry and weep and murmur because of challenges.* Financial goals require plans and for sure you will encounter problems. But, go for them. What I understand about commitment is that with it you cannot fail, with it you will be ready to develop and grow in wisdom, knowledge and understanding. If we are operating in our callings and with our gifts, nothing can stop us. If you start to do anything with your life, be committed to it. *Resolve to stay with your financial goals, training and growth.*

Systemize your financial goals

Part of our business is real estate development and building a house requires technical drawings which guide us to build. Almost all the time, we make some changes to the drawings as we hit the ground but without the initial drawings, we will not have the right measurements and technicalities to produce the building. So are the goals and detailed plans we have; they are flexible and they get updated, we work them as we grow and get more understanding. So will be your financial goals. Have financial goals for yourself and for your business no matter what and commit to them. Write them down, develop steps

> *Dont wait for help or favor*

to reach them and keep reminding yourself of them. That is what I do with my personal life, family life, businesses etc. Be deliberate about this.

Systematize your goals.
A system does not have to be on a computer or on the internet. Develop some steps that will help you to put your finances on automation so that they become independent of your emotions or how you feel in a particular day; whether you are sick, healthy, strong, asleep or awake.

CHAPTER FIVE

FINANCIAL TRAINING

Mistakes! We are going to make them and they can only destroy us when we stop along the way. *When we are obsessed with our vision to building the financial success that we want, we cannot be stopped. We keep going in spite of the challenges and the hurdles we face. If we refuse to continue to train, then our mistakes can overwhelm us.*

> *We should be ready to make thousands of mistakes in the course of living if we want to go beyond average.*

Training is life
What or who trains us has a direct bearing on our results and achievements. We are where we are by what has trained us. Our productivity is as a result of our training. Our work ethics are as a result of how we were trained and so it is with our finances. We have to train for us to get to where we want to go with our finances. Great financial results come out of great financial training.

Discipline is everything. *Our greatest financial wisdom will come from our greatest financial mistakes a lot of the time.* How we handle problems and challenges is because of the training we have undergone. Our training makes us win in life. In this age of social media, we have so many distractions and so many trivialities. We are often occupied with comedy, entertainment, sports, jokes, and religiosities. These if not controlled can take our time and energy. We tend not to focus on things that will bring us financial progress, growth and success.

Skills get results
In our finances, businesses, marriages and other relationships, we will only continue to win when we are committed to the required training. Our entrepreneurship training, sales training, and financial training make us dominate our environment. It is not just about being motivated, but being consciously and properly trained to do what we have to do to win. *Develop the required skillset to get to your goals.* Our results will tell us if we are getting the right training and if we are getting close to our goals. It is good to be motivated, but we have to have a winning strategy and that comes through intentional training. When we focus on training in terms of knowledge and skills, things may not change overnight but we become better to deal with the challenges as they come along. *We need knowledge to turn talent to skill that can create value. The same applies to money; the right financial skill is needed.*

It takes time to move from talent to skill
We are able to spend our time, energy and resources properly when we focus on training, constant acquisition of financial knowledge and constant application of the knowledge acquired.

- Train by reading books.
- Training by watching others do what they do well.
- Train by videos and audios.
- Train by getting into new a network of people who have done what you want to do, who are doing what you are doing and who can stretch you out of your comfort zone.
- Network with those who have the right financial knowledge, skills and results.

Watch how they make their financial decisions. When people are not trained, they get lazy and work becomes a punishment. So are their finances. Your best bet to succeeding is the commitment of your energy to work to get results. It takes hard work and continuous effort, especially when everything seems to be not working. What has trained you will make you fight forward or will make you give up when your finances are in deficit or negative. When you are not getting the desired results, check your training or what has trained you. Business or financial success requires determination. Courage is required. Sometimes, you may feel like giving up but that is not the time to give up. If you don't train, you will not have the required skillset to win.

It is not so much about luck, it is about following the right financial processes and procedures to get the desired results.

It takes work
We achieve our goals when we commit to training. The superstars in any field commit to training. When others are asleep, they are working. They are training. It is no magic. If there is magic at all, it is in the hours and the long hours that they continue to enhance their craft. Any of us can become great if we train enough with our gifts and talents. There is a minimum number of hours of training required for anyone to become an expert in any field. It is not so much about the gift as it is about the commitment to training and development. Achievers know this and they train. *I dare say give yourself a minimum of ten years to train.*

Enjoy this financial training. Whatever we don't know, we can acquire the knowledge and train to get to know it. What others know that we don't know or have that we don't have is because they traded their time to get them. Many people are wishful in their thinking; they are not really resolved to do what has to be done to get the life that they envision for themselves. You commit to train as an entrepreneur in the things that make you better. You train in how to develop better products and services. *You train in sales, prudent financial management, leadership, etc.* These will make your business processes more effective and efficient. If your business succeeds, your finances will succeed as well.

If you are not an entrepreneur, you have to find a way to become so good with your job or career such that if you are not there, they can feel your absence. That is how you add more value to your life and become more valuable.

- Make a difference.
- Don't just show up for the monthly salary.
- Produce results.
- Perform impressively on your job.

The difference is in the training you have had. People think of success but don't like the training process. Have fun with the process too. There is a process before the product.

Become better every day
Entrepreneurship is nothing but constant training to become better at what we do daily. One of the areas that we have to learn to train in is how to get a working business model that is scalable and that is sustainable in the kind of business environment we operate. *Entrepreneurship thrives on creativity and innovation. As much as you can, stay out of government contracts and dealings as a startup and learn to practise with the best of ethics.* It is not a business if you are not proud of your dealings in terms of morals and ethics. *Your business should bring improvement to the society and not to destroy it.* You must have a certain measure of control and predictability in your business. If one person somewhere can stop the flow of money to your business, you don't have

a business.

Cash should flow in multiple inlets. Your business should strive on good management, innovation, system advantages and not on government connections and institutional links as most people do.

The more trained you are with the principles and processes that produce results, the less superstitious you are with your business, finances and business practices. Again, the more control you have over a lot of the activities with your business and finances, the more predictable you are with progress and growth.

The less prepared we are the more fearful we tend to become when we meet challenges with our business finances.

Every business goes through troubles at some point and it is important we keep our calm to get back on track. We can do that well if we stay with the training modules we have when it comes to self-development. If we have to succeed at anything, be it life, career, finances, marriage or business, what we have trained with is a major deciding factor.

The entrepreneur's lifestyle is a constant process of learning. Commit to training and you will succeed. Our finances demand the right financial training. Our career demands that too.

CHAPTER SIX

FINANCIAL GROWTH

Growth diminishes mistakes or has a way of healing debilitating mistakes. *Don't stay at the error level. Leverage your mistakes.* That is a way to correct mistakes made. The best way is never to make them. Unfortunately, mistakes are part of the growth process. Progress comes through pain and mistakes. *Don't run away from mistakes and hope for growth.* I am not talking of negligence or foolishness. Mistakes needed for the journey don't destroy, they build us. Like a child learning to walk, they will fall. That falling is part of the growth process, but if the parent sits there and the child falls from a height and dies, that is not the mistake I am talking about. That is negligence.

Don't live your life being settled with little and only concerned about what you and your family will eat and where your family will sleep. *Financial success is about doing more for society and for people, creating jobs, value and opportunities.* There is so much to do in our country and continent.

The least you can do is to get hooked up to growth and be addicted to expansion.

Expand financially
The way to deal with our pain and mistakes is to expand and get to serve more people and do more out of the experiences and the expertise we gain from our mistakes. Don't think small and don't stay small. Many people get locked up in the financial mistakes they have made and never get over them, and it is largely because of lack of growth. Winning has a way of reducing the pain from mistakes. So no matter what, get over the financial mistakes - the bad loans, the debts, the ones you lost through your greed and the conmen. You have probably become better.

Be hungry for productivity
Life on this earth is in flux. Many people get full with little achievements. They build a house, buy a car and get a job - that is the whole life. They hardly think of what they can do to improve the lives of others. It should not be with our generation. As Africans we should look at what we can do for our Continent and what we have to put in to build the Continent for our children. We don't have the luxury others have. *Our challenges are many and our opportunities are enormous. Let's build our continent, Africa.*

Study Growth There is not much rest from growth. That is why when we get to 10 years, we don't place the growing process on pause before we get to 11 years. Grow emotionally, mentally, spiritually, financially, etc. Think growth and expansion constantly no matter what you do. People quickly get accomplished and satisfied with little. Selfishness is laziness, it is not relativism. There are so many people we can help beyond our families and friends, however, we can only do that when we see growth as important and doing more than what makes us comfortable.

Commit to it
People will accuse you and fight you just because you want to grow and expand yourself, your dream and your passion. Those are people thinking self and little. They will definitely fight you when you decide to become financially successful. It is okay for others to fight you. Don't worry about that. *Worry about you not winning. Go for the win.* Many people get bored when they go on retirement because they lose their drive, and reason they must do more to help others. Once they get another purpose, they become rejuvenated and vibrant. Take care of your finances before you get to retirement. Plan for that future. Aging is certain, but financial success calls for passion, innovation, problem solving, constant planning and thinking.

Money fuels vision
Growth feeds on money to a large extent. *Study money and how to get it, keep it and grow it.* No matter your passion or what you want to become, money is the fuel to that vision.

Study it. Money is a tool. Learn it. Money is a skill. Get it. They say that the best way to help the poor, is to learn not to be one of them. It is a lot easier if your knowledge on finances are a bit close to accurate and your emotions about money and the decisions that are made around it are sound. *When we identify ourselves, we identify our purpose and our abilities and our desire to help others does not stop.* That requires a growth mindset. I think we need more than the content of our degrees to do anything significant with our lives. For us to succeed we need courage, the ability to take risk, persistence, commitment, adaptability, and continuous learning. It is difficult to realize our dreams by following the social script - go to school, get a job, marry, have children, and put them to school to repeat the same cycle.

Secondary or first degree level of education is enough start for financial success. *There are so many people with no education who are rich.* But most people are largely fixated on getting lots of degrees even though they don't need them in the line of their career. Even if you don't pay the fees, you will use your time to get those degrees.

Focus on productivity and taking more responsibilities to get results than just getting degrees for your financial success. Looking at our continent, where we are and where we want to go, I believe more than 80% of our resources should be geared towards creativity, innovation and entrepreneurship. That is the way we are going to solve a lot of our problems concerning housing, healthcare, education, sanitation, food, clothing, water, energy, data, media, etc. *We need a lot of creative minds who are prepared for the next level.* This is where huge financial success resides. Let us reduce the passion for sports, entertainment, religious activities, politics, etc. I don't think we have the luxury to enjoy what those without our basic problems of unemployment, waste, lack of factories, healthcare, food, housing, etc., enjoy.

Financial growth
You cannot play big if you don't see the value high quality people bring. The way I see big players is that they are self-driven. They share. *They think beyond self. They think big.* Financial success has a lot to do with creation with a vision. It starts with hustling. Beyond that, we start to think structurally. We have a lot of corporate executives teaching financial success, but for most of us, it will take entrepreneurship. Learn from those who are doing it and doing it big. We only fail when we give up. Growth is constant. We have got to love what we do. *Go for growth.* Growth is supposed to be a natural phenomenon, but it requires directed effort. So is our financial life. *Grow mentally, spiritually, emotionally, financially, and socially as well.*

Don't wait for help. Be that help
Develop your people skills because growth requires leadership, and being an entrepreneur demands persistence

and stability. No excuses.

Our dream of financial prosperity requires the same persistence. As much as we have been told about what God can do for us and what God does for us, we cannot wait for God to do the things that we are responsible to change. Let God rather count on us to change things for the better. There are too many educated religious African youth waiting and praying to God to solve our problems for us. If anything, I think God expects us to change our finances for the better. Don't follow miracles for growth. Follow principles.

Organization brings development and growth and so financial success requires organization. If we don't practise what is orderly, it will be hard to see growth. Success they say is not an accident. Success is purposeful. If you see anybody successful financially, they were intentional about it somewhere along the line. They wanted to succeed. They thought about it. They talked about it. They walked with like-minded people. They worked the success. Same if we want financial growth; we have to want it, we have to desire it and we have to work it. Use time and work to get financial growth. Stretch it. Demand it. Go for financial growth.

CHAPTER SEVEN

MONEY EQUALITY

When we talk about women equality, I believe it should largely start with financial equality. You can only control somebody when you have control over their mind, time and money. When women have money they have a say. They have options. My best advice to women is to own their money. Create your own wealth, no matter how small it is. Sell something. Do business. Start somewhere. Beyond that think of employing people.

> *When women have their own money and control of their own money, they can control a lot in life, especially African women.*

Don't wait for a miracle to get money
What creates riches are the financial systems we have developed ourselves. Money is a derivative of financial structures. The financial skills, attitude and character we have used our time to develop, have a lot to do with the amount of money we can produce and multiply.

We get money by the economic problems we solve. Money is not a miracle, it is not from prayer and fasting, and definitely not from anointing oil or all night breakthrough meetings as they have made it seem in Africa for Christians. Money is a product of economic productivity.

Don't leave your financial life and future to anybody. It is our own responsibility.

Think again

Financial independence is that important and we don't achieve it by wishful thinking. It requires deliberate, systemic and long term planning and work.

- Money is one thing that people have to make a lot of decisions around.

- Money is that important to running your family, health, education and children's education, residence etc. Yet people don't take that much time to study it.

Most people have been conditioned to think looking rich is being rich, but that is not so. *Your salary is not for eating.* Your salary is about the first step to building a secure financial future. Every one of us has something to start with in building the financial freedom he or she wants. Your salary is for that starting point. A lot of people think they are poor and that they have no chance or nothing to start with; that is simply not true. We all have something to start with;

we have friends, energy, time, endurance, persistence, etc. I think what is usually the problem is our ignorance - not knowing what to do and believing that we are disadvantaged. *No matter the job you have, the salary you receive or where you live, if you so desire to become better financially, you can become.* It is a matter of knowing what to do from where you are with what you have. It starts with believing that you can become better financially. You only need the right mindset, skillset and tools and create the right environment. Many have been programmed to get money to spend and not to have a well thought-out plan to follow into that financial future. *Most of us have no financial goal or plan. We just are surviving each day hoping that one day one day, things will just change. Things don't change like that. Not your finances.*

Think wild and wide
The world system has programmed us to think little and small when it comes to finances and how money is created or made. I think that many people will not be able to build businesses that will make them successful because they are not ready to go through what it takes to build successful companies which can make them wealthy. It takes a lot of effort and sacrifices, but because a lot of people get some sort of income, even if it is not enough, they can be financially free if they work it.

Have a plan for what comes in and look at how more than one source can bring in money to you. That is why you don't have to take for granted where that income is coming from. People think when they work, they work for somebody but you get a salary and that is what you can also use to build the financial future you want. If you have good financial goals and you are able to follow them through, you will be fine.

- Don't take for granted the job that you have that gets you some kind of income.
- Talk well of the company or the job and be truthful there.
- Don't be the one who is wishing the company will fail
- Don't be the one stealing from the company.

If you are an entrepreneur, pay those who work with you well and don't take them for granted. Talk to them with respect and openness. Let them feel happy working with you and inspire them to become the best. Some will go to start their own businesses, give them the best of support. Our knowledge on money and wealth should be different and we must learn from the best. Everyone can stay out of basic money problems if they get the right knowledge on money.

Connect with great people
I believe when you find a good person to work with, don't trash or trivialize the relationship. *Our people hardly link their financial success with their networks.* That is why people hardly get financially ahead, particularly employees who are always changing jobs. They believe there is a job somewhere that will make them rich. No, it is the network you are able

to build over time with good people who understand money and have money. What you are able to learn from them makes a huge difference. When you pick your phone, how many of your contacts have money and how many can you call and will call you back. Financial proximity is a decider. *You can decide to be with people for a long haul through thick and thin.* If you cannot build a company then, be with people who are building companies and investments while you are still employed by them. What I see is that people don't stay with such people with the intention of being part of the dream and wealth building so by the time things work out, the relationship is over. One of the reasons most people stay poor all their lives or struggle all their lives in terms of finances is that they are not able to stay connected with such networks.

From my observation, we have had most of our information on finances from people who have not really created wealth. They usually look rich until they are in their 60s or when they are on retirement. That is the time you get to know that the people we call middle-class are not solid in finances. Every one of us can build from where we are. You can even be selling on your head, you can still start from there.

There is the need for workable financial knowledge
Take your financial knowledge from those who are rich or building financial empires. You can be employed and still build other sources of revenue without stealing from the

company.

You can stay honest and ethical and still build wealth. What is important is, you are building your knowledge and seeing it as a way to financial independence. Depending on your level, you can always learn to build extra income sources or investments from real estate rentals, cash crops, royalties, investments in other people's businesses etc.

Instead of you trying to buy land and build a house from one source of income, why don't you have a plan of say 5 years and put that money to start a cocoa farm or something that can grow the money first before you build that house. Always think of multiplying the money before you use it to build or buy a house or a car when it's not excess money.

This will take time and it will take different thinking and lifestyle. Not everyone wants to build a business but everyone can build an investment. *Everyone can be financially independent if they put their mind to it.* However, this requires sacrifices.

Study cash flow
You can look at cash flow on any investment you do for the future such as real estates, cash crops, etc. You the investor must have knowledge in what you are doing. Again, self-development is the best of investments. *Invest in yourself before you invest in anything.* If you don't know it or understand it, you are likely to lose it. So invest in knowledge first.

If you don't have billions, then you have to understand cash flow on any business or investment you get involved in. How is the money coming in and how is the money going out and at what time difference? Always sit down to calculate. It will save you from a lot of pain and frustration. Don't just take the contract because it is a big contract. *Do your numbers.* How much do you need to start, when do they pay and at what time intervals? That is why even little businesses who see money every day seem to do better than most contract businesses that are always chasing payments which never come on time. *You have to make a conscious effort to learn about finances and how wealth is created. You can be a struggling business person all your life because you refuse to learn about money.* The knowledge to create financial success must be sought if it's not readily available. Don't put up with lack and poverty. Set goals to be financially wealthy if you want to be financially independent.

Pursue financial freedom as well.
Just as going to school and looking for employment has been imbibed in our psyche, becoming prosperous must also be imbibed in our psyche for us to work towards a better financial future. *If you don't have any connection with financially successful people - be they family or friends - your understanding of how money is created is cladded.*
You will believe that getting degrees and getting a good-paying job will get you there. This is not accurate. I usually see people working and developing themselves who then stop the work and go back to school hoping that when they get more degrees, they will get promoted, have their salary

increased and get financially free. Ask those who did that if it has really made any difference.

Very few disciplines of life take a lot of degrees to succeed and even that, not financially. Those are special technical areas that are highly regulated. That which brings progress is deliberate self-development, whether you went to school or not.

Create your own prosperity
Don't wait for another person to discover you. If that has not happened all this while, what makes you think it will? At a certain point, degrees and certificates have very little to creating financial freedom. Our brothers and sisters who are selling on the street make some income which they can build business with.

Proper financial knowledge, skill and discipline is the way to create financial freedom. Making money has a lot to do with resilience. There will be many hurdles from your own self-doubt and all the problems that society and others will bring your way the moment you decide to go for financial freedom. But don't quit. Go for it. Each and every one of us is responsible for our financial success and freedom. Choose that path. There is equity, and there is equality. It is our power to choose.

CHAPTER EIGHT

☙

FAMILY AND FINANCIAL EDUCATION

The person you get to marry has tremendous effect on your financial success and peace in life.

In dividuals who are able to build great financial successes and marriages seem to have spouses who have some confidence in them even in their wildest and stupid moments even if both had to start with little. They seem to have partners who are mesmerized by their intelligence and heart to work. *You don't need your wife or husband to compete with you or constantly express doubt in your decisions.*

That is a burden. Not many people have these kinds of spouses or are able to build up such unions. It's the reason why business, financial and marital successes hardly happen at the same time. It is a difficult work, especially without the right understanding and tools. *You have to work to have a peaceful, fulfilling and financially successful marriage or family.* It is work and it takes deliberate effort to build a marriage or family that is peaceful and prosperous. *Marriage is not the end in itself, it is a means to productivity, purpose and achieving something more significant than if the two had not married.* Most of our men don't know how to build anything productive with their wives. In fact, most don't support their women to have economic power. You don't have to think like that. Marriage takes both of you working together. Family is a team. You have to be on one page. Work to help each other to succeed. Work to succeed together. That is the essence of love; wanting the best for you both.

Family is foundational
Marriage is a very intimate yet vulnerable relationship. What is said by one means a lot to the others. Make it a resolution to build each other up because a family or marriage is a company which runs with vision and finance. The state of the finances of most families is the deciding point of most of the other issues in the marriage. *How the finances are handled has a lot to show on the peace and happiness in the marriage.* You will have to be determined to build the financial knowledge required to lift the family particularly when you are building a family and business at the same time. The challenges are many. You get better as you become skilled. The advice for the family where both spouses are in business is different from the family where both spouses are employed or one is employed and the other is an entrepreneur and so forth. *The sacrifices required are very different in each situation.*

The mindset of a rich family seems to be focused on creating multiple avenues of revenue and they learn to build the capacity to increase their cash flows all the time because that is how wealth is built. On the other hand, the mindset of the poor family is likely to be focused on acquiring cars and houses to tell others that they are rich or have arrived. The difference between the rich and the poor families show very well when they get to their pension ages where they don't get paid and the health bills go up. That is the point we get to know the wisdom in building investments which can bring in cash at the time that we cannot physically do so.

Love is not destructive
Don't live and expect another person to take care of you when you are on pension. That is a bad choice or decision. It goes to show that you were not in charge of your finances.

Even if your spouse is risk averse, you can still help him or her to develop because he or she can identify some things that you may not see had the two of you not discussed.

You have a better chance of success as a couple when you make a decision to both grow intellectually and emotionally together. *Every human grows on genuine love. No one will throw away authentic love.* So learn to love one another. Love always wins. Build that financial future together. Involve each other and appreciate each other.

Entrepreneurs' love story.
The entrepreneurs' love story is unique because there is constant pressure both on the family and the business that you are building, especially at the initial stages. The sacrifices are enormous and countless. We deal with a lot of challenges like any other family where both are entrepreneurs with growing children. Every family is special and will be successful if you commit to continuous learning and development together at every stage of the process.

- Love is not blind.
- Love is light.
- Love is knowledge.
- Love is wisdom.

Don't underestimate the capacity of your woman or your man and what you can achieve together if you put your minds together towards any goal. *Read together. Train together. Build together.*

You need skills to build a peaceful and successful marriage.
Try to read the same books, listen to the same audios and watch videos on finances. This is how to stay at the same wavelength on a lot of issues. *You create problems when you refuse to grow together, especially in knowledge.*

As a man, love your wife. Study your wife. Support and encourage her to build her life. The same advice applies to women. Adore him. You will only reap the investment you both make in each other. Be a man; and a man must not be broke all the time. Be that man who is not broke all the time. *Have some money and courage and be stable for your wife and children.* You are the foundation and you are responsible for the mess and the mistakes. You will have peace if you don't make her responsible for the mess but the victories and the successes.

An understanding of marriage processes will give you the capacity to handle the pressures and the difficulties of marriage as a man. *Don't run away from the troubles and from your duties.* Stay when the pressure is on. This does not apply to everyone. You can have a lot of peace as a man if you can put things in perspective. You are responsible for the family, the finances, the security, etc.

Shower love and affection on your woman. She never gets tired of it. She is precious and special, priceless and delicate. Take good care of her. It is that beautiful to have a happy and joyful woman in your life. It takes work. These things require money and that is why we have to get our finances in good shape. We must work at it every day to become better. Family is everything you make it. Work to create the best of environment for your children as well; an environment where everyone is learning to become better and more confident and more inspired to do more. Prosper together. Love never fails.

CHAPTER NINE

SELL FOR FINANCIAL FREEDOM

One of the ways to get extra income in our country is to start to sell something that people need. There are so many provision shops all over and lots of shops which sell all kinds of products. Starting to retail does not require a lot of capital or skills and for me, it is one of the ways to get income or extra income.

Many families in our country depend on these shops for their livelihood.

Whenever I look at those who sell on the streets, their passion and how they are able to convince their customers, I see that selling is the way to get money. Not many people get the dynamics and the alacrity they use to sell on the street. Money is not in the classroom, it is in selling. *If you cannot sell, market, brand, promote, negotiate and sometimes fight, then you are going to struggle as an entrepreneur.*

You have to master them. They are learnable. Selling is income they say. Most people look down on sales especially those in our markets or those we call informal because most people who have not come close to selling in our markets don't seem to understand the numbers. You want to learn to be an entrepreneur or start a business, then start to look at what you can sell, be it product or service. *It is not that easy for people to approach others to sell anything to them.*

Acquiring this is a great business skill. I understand it is very tough for most people with higher education to go into selling because their mates, friends, and families will make them feel like they have failed or wasted their time going to the university only to end up selling. You really have to have a tough mind to start to sell your services or products to people when things don't look that structured in the beginning.

You have got to learn how to sell products and services and how to negotiate and ask for what you have to ask, or it will be difficult to pick yourself up. *People think that if we have been to school, we don't have to learn how to sell anything.* It is one of the ways to start building a business for extra income. We just have to learn how to sell, negotiate and convince. Again, learn to sell because it is part of the foundation of being successful at anything we set out to do. Selling is required in almost everything that we have to do to become successful. Convincing anyone to agree with you takes some selling abilities. *Politicians have to sell themselves and hope the people vote for them.* To get a partner, you have to sell to the person what he or she is going to get by agreeing to walk with you.

Selling is one of the easiest ways to get revenue to fund your business idea or your vision. It is also about the skill that comes to us at the initial stages of us trying to build any dream. Anything that we have to get in exchange of another is a form of selling. It can be a product or service or an idea that we want people to be part of.

If you can learn to sell, you will go to places. The leverage of technology in sales is so enormous. Phone calls, social media, videos etc. can all help us to sell. Social media is a tool that is helping many in selling their services or products. You don't have to be a technical person and have a skill in coding or software development to use these applications. *This is the time we live in now - Facebook, WhatsApp, Instagram etc.* People are always on their phones and you can target the people who will need the products you are selling.

Selling is a skill that can be developed with the right training. So many young women are selling all kinds of things with these social media apps. What they may need to add are proper team building skills, customer service and financial management skills and their businesses will take shape. Others are rebranding or repacking existing products and selling them over the internet.

Again, remember sales is income. Look at the agriculture industry, the retail industry, the technology industry, construction, education industry, health industry, sports industry, entertainment industry, etc.; what can you sell if you look at each of these value chain, products or services?

Make a decision to learn about sales and the processes attached to sales. This includes how to close sales, how to up sell, cross sell and down sell, and how to handle objections. Don't let your school or lack of it be an impediment to you learning to sell yourself. Whatever we manufacture or produce will have to be sold and to even build a business, it is far better to learn how the products are going to be sold before you start to produce them.

Everyone is selling something. Most people are not aware though. We sell as individuals and we sell with our teams. Training is so important to being able to sell to many with good margins. How we handle customers' objections, good customer service and understanding the culture of our customers are very important. *Learn to handle the nos.* You will hear so many people saying no when you start to sell your product to them. Continue to hear the nos. It is just a stage. As you build, you will become better and your business will gather momentum and that is where you will start to see success. Selling is money.
Don't forget that. *You don't have money because you cannot*

sell. We need to study sales and teach our teams too. In our retail outlets, we continually train our teams to be more productive. So intentionally learn about how you can use sales to support your finances, build a business or an extra source of income.

CHAPTER TEN

HOUSE OWNERSHIP AND YOUR FINANCES

People get so much interested and a bit emotional when it comes to owning a house or building one. We attach financial success to owning a house or houses and truth be told, it takes a lot of money to build or buy a house. If we look at our salary levels and what it costs to build a two or three bedroom house, most people will need to plan very well to be able to own their own house. This is largely because the technology and the materials we are using to build our houses cost a lot - the cement, the irons, the roofing and the finishing.

And there is this thinking that renting a house is not such a good idea, I think otherwise.

If you are a business person or building wealth, then you have to know how to apportion your money when it comes to anything that calls for a lot of money like building a house or buying one.

For instance, if I rent a two bedroom house for say GH¢500 a month, a year will be GH¢6000 but if I were to build that house, at least it will be around say GH¢200,000 conservatively. Now if I am building a business or wealth, I think it will be more prudent to rent for a while and put that money in the business. This money which is the GH¢ 200,000 minus the rent (GH¢194,000) should multiply to about GH¢1,000,000 before taking that much money to build a house or buy, if that house is not going to be rented out for income. *This is for those who don't have much but are hopeful to create a financially independent future.*

Financial education for an entrepreneur is different from individual finance. *Overcoming poverty is different from creating wealth. Both require different sets of knowledge and skill. One is defending and the other wants to score.* We have got to think differently and make the right financial choices. *Everyone pays rent, whether the house owned or rented. If you own the house, you still spend to maintain it, get it insured, pay property tax, etc.* Building a great future requires financial decisions on investments that will continue to bring in money now and the future. Thus a lot of our choices should be geared towards building those investments. Investing in businesses, properties, cash crop farming, etc. should be considered. *This will require a plan, a system and commitment to follow it through*; at least a 10-20 year plan to create that financial future that you will be proud of. *The best of investment starts with financial education.*

You need to have your values rightly set because most people compromise their values when it comes to money. You don't need to be corrupt to achieve this. You only need a system in place. That is what we will talk about in our next chapter.

CHAPTER ELEVEN

STREAMLINE YOUR FINANCES

The world financial systems have been designed to keep most people average or poor all their lives. Many will go to school to become lawyers, doctors, engineers, accountants, teachers, police officers, nurses, etc. *They will hardly understand the financial systems that operate in their country.* Look at the salary levels, taxes, interests on loans, etc. People use their time to study everything but the financial systems of their country.

Most educated people think that the way to get money is through salary. That is their best understanding of money and this is why they work for it all their lives and never still have any. You don't have to wish the financial system will make you financially independent. It was not designed to do that. It was designed to take from you and not to give to you. It takes a system to fight a system to win and that is why you have to have your own financial system that will work automatically for your financial freedom.

Put in place a financial system designed to multiply your money and protect it

A system does not need you to be present for it to work. It works automatically and only requires maintenance and attention once a while. We have to know that we are responsible for our finances and our financial future. This system should be able to take care of your income, expenses, savings, budgeting, cash flow, etc. It does not have to be on a computer per se. It can be done with a paper and pen. It is possible to have a system where you don't have to spend more than say 20% of your total wealth to buy or build a house or say 10% to buy a car.

Design your own financial system.
Ideally, it should be a 10-30 year financial plan and must have the following elements

- Saving money every month
- Multiplying what is saved
- At what times can those be accessed
- What returns will come in monthly
- When to spend any bulk money on cars, houses etc.
- Family expenses, children's school fees
- Insurance and health issues etc.
- The assets and how they grow in value
- How much wealth will be created over the 10-30 year duration.

You can design yours totally differently from this. What is important is achieving the goals, that is, being aware of you having your own financial system and it working as desired. Systematize your money. Don't leave it to chance. No one is responsible but you. School was not designed to make you rich. The best it can do is to help you overcome acute poverty. But School is a great tool which inspires and equips the mind to create the future we want.

Mainly we have to educate ourselves financially to become financially successful.

AFTERWORD

I hope you have picked something on money that will make your financial future a bit brighter. Money plays a huge role in this life and those who understand this and work towards it don't have the same problems that majority of the people (who spend all their lives struggling with money or lack money) have. Financial education is imperative if we are going to achieve our financial goals and it is in a constant learning state. If the process is wrong, the product will be wrong. Most Africans believe that to be financially successful, they have to travel outside the continent. This idea is faulty.

Find your own life purpose and what you can do to help Africa develop. Study money religiously as well. Keep your values at a very high level. You don't need to become a thief to have money. Help as many people as possible. Look at the problems you can solve. Share your discoveries with others. Finally, build your own financial system. Thank you for taking time to read this book.

NOTES

NOTES

Made in the USA
Las Vegas, NV
17 June 2025